MW00736928

Finding
My
Way

poems by David Mello

*To the Folks
at Farmington Station
All the Best.*

David Mello

Pidgeon Loft Press
West Hartford CT

Pidgeon Loft Press
PO Box 270603
West Hartford CT 06127-0603
azorean.9@gmail.com

ISBN: 978-0-692-74073-6

This book is dedicated to Nugget
My Little Buddy
I miss you so

NUGGET

CONTENTS

I // Seasons 15

II // Romance and Love 25

III // Home, Family and Friends 43

IV // About Pets   71

V // Sports and Music   79

VI // The Struggle 103

VII // World Order 125

My Little Smokey Boy

Jumps on the table.
Jumps on the chair.
Jumps everywhere
He doesn't care.

My very first poem
(Clifton, New Jersey, 1994)

Acknowledgements

To my lovely wife Diane for all your encouragement and continued support. You gave me strength when I faltered. I greatly appreciate the many hours you devoted to the editing process and help with selecting the pictures. I especially enjoyed your creative touch in the setting for the photo you produced for Section V. Most importantly I am grateful for your interest in my writing, indeed you are my muse. My love for you stretches far beyond the universe.

To Joseph Keeney the book shepherd, who provided guidance through the process and made it happen for me.

To my buddy and fellow poet Andy Weil who introduced me to the Faxon Poetry Group rekindling my interest in writing.

To my friend and fellow poet June Mandelkern who shared her experience and knowledge helping me to envision the big picture.

Love is what matters and life is for now.

Excerpt from the poem, *A Day in the Journey*.
David Mello, May 16, 2011

Forward

My poetry is of the people. Simple and from the heart. A baby boomers perspective on life and the world around us. I am a story-teller and touch upon a variety of subjects. My intent is to immerse myself in the verse and in the meaning it conveys, hoping the reader identifies with the poem and is in some way moved with emotion.

My work has been published in Perspectives VI (2012), Perspectives VII (2013), Perspectives VIII (2014), Perspectives IX (2015), Perspectives X (2016) - Faxon Poets, West Hartford, CT and the Long River Run (2012) - Connecticut Poetry Society, Hartford, CT.

I can't change the destination of the wind, but I can adjust my sails to always reach my destination. ~Jimmy Dean

Introduction

I was born in the south end waterfront district of New Bedford, Massachusetts. The son of Manuel Mello Jr. a manufacturing manager and Maria Helena Botelho a seamstress. I am a second generation American. My paternal and maternal grandparents emigrated from the Island of Sao Miguel in the Portuguese Azores.

As a youth I attended parochial elementary school in New Bedford through the eighth grade. In 1966 I graduated from New Bedford High School. I attended the University of Massachusetts at Dartmouth, graduating in 1970 with a B.S. in Business Administration.

My early professional years saw me working in retail clothing and the toy industry. Subsequently moving to the on-line Internet world as a buyer of computer products.

While attending college I became interested in poetry but did not take up the pen seriously until many years later while living in Austin, Texas. After living in the Southwest for nine years I returned to New England in the spring of 2010 and settled in West Hartford, Connecticut with my wife Diane, dog Annie Girl and cats Little Voice and Jelly Red.

Poetery is an echo, asking a shadow to dance. ~ Carl Sandburg

I
SEASONS

Tell Me Where the Flowers Are

There are no flowers here today -
nor any buds at all.
Abandoned without care.
The garden sleeps through winter months
of cold and snowy days.

The colors are all gone.
No one comes along.
Quiet solitude prevails,
awaiting life to come.

The days of early spring
will melt the snow away.
Then all will come to life.
Buds will bloom again.

I cannot see the colors now,
the old man says to me.
His eyes do not work so well
but he expects to see -
pretty colors in the garden
where he likes to be.

His mind is truly sound
and his memory is clear.
He asks one thing of me -
in the days of bright sunshine,
Please take me to the garden walk,
and tell me where the flowers are.

Those Sunny Days

We opened up our roadside stand
    for another summer season.
Just five miles from Horsenack Beach
    near Westport by the sea.

We loaded up with paper bags
    at fifty to a bundle.
Packed wooden crates with corn
    and stacked them on the tables.

Driving from the shore,
    cars lined up on Slocum Road
stopping off to buy a bag
    of our home grown country corn.

We greeted every buyer
    with a beaming friendly smile.
I remember well those sunny days.
    Our corn was king in summertime.

After the Rain

A heavy rain falls this morning
on New York's city streets.
Parades of black umbrellas march
to the sounds of sloshing feet.

Curbside puddles splash up
from cars along the way.
Lots of rainwear fashion
are walking on display.

Sitting in a coffee shop -
a waitress brings me breakfast.
I look out beyond the window
at the frenzied sidewalk traffic.

The morning race continues
on the concrete track below.
The masses will soon vanish.
For eight hours, they will go.

Autumn Chill

In amber woods on gray fall days,
I take my walk in morning haze.
The mist will lift before too long
on yonder path I'll stroll along.

With passing thoughts I make my way
there are many deeds to do this day.
What beauty here these woods unfold
so crisp the air, so fresh and bold.

Dappled sunlight shining through.
The sky now clears in vibrant blue.
The woods turn quiet and very still.
Surrounding me in autumn chill.

A Winter Day in Boston

Snow falls softly on Beacon Hill.
This historic neighborhood
of gas lit lanterns,
cobblestone streets,
all covered in white.
A scene of postcard quality.

The muffled sounds of Acorn Street
produce a comforting quiet.
From a nearby bench he feeds some birds.
The small bag of seed is well received.
It's a cold day for these feathered friends.

He thinks about his evening plans
with a lady he met at the bookstore.
Celtics tickets for the Garden,
dinner reservations
at Figs on Charles Street.

He returns to his office,
attends a late afternoon meeting,
bringing Friday to a close.
He looks forward to his evening;
on this winter day in Boston.

Snow Falls Today

Where does the sparrow fly
on this cold December day.
Through a broken window pane
at the barn on Mellows Way.

Snow is falling heavy now.
Roads and roofs deep in white.
A horse drawn sleigh is drawing near,
bringing friends to stay the night.

Our fireplace roars with burning logs -
yellow flames and embers glow.
The steady fire removes the chill -
so dog and man are warmer still.

The snow will stop sometime soon
if not tonight for sure by noon.
We end the evening sipping wine,
with music soft to sooth the mind.

Winters Grip

Is it springtime now?
The calendar tells us so.
But take a look around.
Is that snow there on the ground?
Today is cold and gray
and more snow is on the way.

April has arrived.
But it doesn't mean a thing.
We have yet to see
a single sign of spring.

We need to break the grip
and change from cold to warm.
This winter lingers on
like a boring marathon.

II
ROMANCE
and
LOVE

Number 112

Have you ever seen a garden with buds all abloom
or looked up in the sky at an eagle spread in flight?
A display of fulfillment and freedom is what you see.
A feeling of glee comes over me.

Through the years you show me kindness.
You care from deep within your soul.
A soothing vision with those flowers in your hair,
your long skirts fluttering in the breeze.

I have entered the borders of your circle
in pursuit of an open heart.
Difficult to bear is this burden of doubt
such is the challenge we follow.

The road to love exposed to the winds of chance
or guided by destiny, should you be so lucky.
The trueness of life forever elusive,
be soft and kind to its approach
forever tender to its touch.

My Jersey Rose

In the Garden State I found a rose.
A lovely flower that touched my life.
I plucked this flower and held it close.
One day this rose became my wife.

That glowing smile on a face so fair,
a striking contrast to her auburn hair.
This stunning beauty of glamour and grace
stands by my side in her own space.

Her hearty laughter lightens the load
making our home such a happy abode.
Her fiery spirit ignites the air.
She looks after me with tender care.

Her engaging mind and snapping wit
can lift you up – just a bit!
Her soothing touch does comfort me
and the fire of her form still keeps me warm.

Most of all – I am blessed to know
that in this life – I am loved by her.

     Indeed you are
         My Jersey Rose

Dance with Me

Behold the days of youthful love;
when flowers were in bloom.
Our summertime had just begun.
It was the month of June.

I met a girl, a lovely lass
with eyes of emerald green.
Her hair was red, a fiery red.
Such hair I'd never seen.

She turned her head
and smiled at me.
I buckled at the knee.

I looked at her
and then I said,
Will you dance with me?

We stepped out on the dance floor.
I held her hand in mine.
For a moment I stood breathless.
To me she was divine.

We waltzed around in circles -
doing twirls and fancy spins.
My heart was beating faster.
Then I began to grin.

Her freckled face was beaming.
She indeed enjoyed the dance.
The balance of this evening,
will be left to fate and chance.

Meeting Diane

The rain was heavy that night
driving along old 9W
on my way to Fort Lee.

My destination –
a restaurant called THE BICYCLE CLUB.

I arrived on time but remained in my car
pondering how I would navigate running
between the large raindrops.

I dashed through the parking lot,
stepping in every puddle
on my way to the door.

Entering, I saw a lady sitting at a table –
Instantly, I knew that was her.
I walked over, sat down and introduced myself.

She looked marvelous.
Such a lovely smile.
An amber eyed beauty she was.

We talked some.
Ordered a cocktail,
followed by dinner.

The evening went well
but ended all too quickly.
It was soon time to say goodnight.

That's how it all began.
With me and Diane.

You and Me

Let's enter the valley
of uncertainty.
Follow me into eternity.
Holding my hand
we will take a stand
for what we believe.

We can go the distance -
you and me.
It will be wonderful
just wait and see.
We will make our happiness,
nurture our love and watch it bloom.

How lucky we are
for what we have found.
So much to enjoy
when we look around.

We will capture the moon
the sun and the sea.
We will do it together –
just you and me.

Our Time

Warm kisses I remember,
from that long ago September.
How nice it was to be with you,
to hold you close, feel you near.
Our love was new and filled with wonder.

Fate dealt us an unkind hand
of time and place and circumstance.
Our struggle was to understand.
Young, confused and overwhelmed,
undone we stood and came apart.

Feeling hopeless against the odds
a sad emptiness came over us.
With broken hearts our ship did sail.
Our sky turned dark from the fading sun.
Our days grew long and very cold.

After many years we meet again.
The chance of fate reversed, now kind.
Such joy I feel at seeing you.
Do you feel the same when you look at me?
What was lost has now been found.

We can now get back, within our time,
our misplaced love of yesterday.
Step forward with your lovely smile.
Reach out and take my hand.
Come with me to forever land.

One Dance

Thoughts of you
became a song.
I wrote the lyrics
and the melody.

Stay with me
on this cold December day.
Curl up by the fire
and love the night away.

The wind howls,
snow is piling up.
The roads are not clear.
There is no place to go.

Much time has passed
since our last encounter.
I remember well
that long happy day.

Nothing stays the same,
how it ends we don't know.
I'm happy I was close to you,
the music was wonderful -
but we only had one dance.

Here's a lucky stone.
Take it when you go.
Keep it with you,
next to your heart.

The Gift

We share our lives now.
From where we've come,
to where we are and
beyond to where we'll be.

From Austin to Boston
and all points in-between.
We are truly blessed
to have each other near.

We embrace the rising sun,
and dream of our tomorrows.
We'll be here for each other,
with love in every way.

Walking through the journey.
Holding hands together
each and every day,
is the only gift we need.

The Brightness of Tomorrow

Like the sun that follows rain.
Good times replace bad.
Kindness eases pain.
Happy overcomes sad.

Just lean on me a while,
let me hold you close.
Take comfort
in the warmth of my embrace.

Our courage will help us
rise above the ashes.
Storms always pass,
calmness will prevail.

We will look to the future
and set our path forward.
Today's darkness will give way
to the brightness of tomorrow.

Still In Love

Even though we stumbled
our time together matters.
We said some unkind things
but words will fade away.

Hold me close, stay with me,
our love will overcome.
Let's talk about tomorrow
and watch the sun come up.

The world will keep on spinning
no matter what we do.
I've listened to my heart today.
I'm still in love with you.

We Are Texans

Some promises are hard to keep.
Even those we make from love.
We loosen our grip on yesterday
to hold on for tomorrow.

We believe in what we planned.
From the sand dunes of old Cape Cod
to the Hill Country of central Texas.
We make the journey and share our hearts.

Our eyes open to this new land.
The culture and people so different.
Here we unravel the mystery of our souls.
A strong dependence on each other
takes root in our need to survive.

We promise not to be here forever
far away from our dear New England.
So we engage and adapt,
assimilating to the world around us.

Growing closer every day.
Learning about each other.
Living out the journey.
We have love and make our own happiness.
For a while we are Texans.

To Love Again

In the wind I hear a whisper –
a voice calling me.
My mind filled with memories.
I am a haunted man.

Misfortune came our way.
You left my arms too soon.
I struggle with my days and
fight the nightly demons.

I keep staring at the stars –
a frozen posture of anticipation.
Waiting for a sign from beyond
my heart beats with a rhythm of hope.

Loving You Today

I remember well the time of my youth,
the awesome beauty of yesteryear.
Days of aging are upon me now.
Meeting them with resistance,
I struggle with the reality of life.

I look at you –
you are my greatest love.
Talk to me, I am listening.
Tell me you will always love me.

Let me hold you on this autumn day.
Feel the fire and passion
that still burns in my being.
You are an endless beauty
with a heart and soul of gold.

I shall never tire of you.
It's late in the evening,
we need to make our way home,
put some logs in the fireplace
and love away the night.

The Ride

That old man in the mirror
sure looks a lot like me.
Many years have added up
and stocked my memory.

My youthful days are cloudy,
the sun no longer strong.
My friends have disappeared
there's no one to tag along.

With some people in the park
I play a game I never liked.
It helps to pass the time
then I walk or take a hike.

At night I have some dinner
with a glass of wine or two.
It used to be so nice
when it was me and you.

Now I go on alone
with your spirit at my side.
Your presence never stronger -
let's go for a ride.

A Song for Magdalena

In San Antone I met a lady
in the square by the Alamo.
Her hair was brown her eyes were too -
a taunting figure in a modest dress.

I stopped to chat that summer day.
I knew right then we'd take a stroll -
by the River Walk in the Texas sun.
Hand in hand, we walked along.

With the voice of an angel
and her haunting smile,
I was intrigued and lost for words.
My heart beat fast that afternoon.

Clouds cleared as we made the turn.
The threat of rain was never real.
Our sun shone bright from that day on,
the day that turned our lives around.

We found ourselves a lasting love.
Strength of self gave us reason
to go on and believe in each other.
Looking back from life's other side
I sing a song for Magdalena.

III
HOME,
FAMILY
and
FRIENDS

My Home Town

On this grey day I was alone,
took a ride and went back home;
olde New Bedford by the sea
that fishing town was calling me.

I found myself on Homers Wharf
across the way from Freestones Bar.
I grabbed a spot to rest a bit,
a wooden bench where I could sit.

Lobster pots stacked on high,
why they don't tip you wonder why.
Native gulls fly all around
screeching their familiar sound.

Fishing boats are quite a sight
packed and jammed so close and tight.
Their masts are tall and strung with nets.
Wharf rats dance across their decks.

Upon their rusted bows you see
familiar names of family.
Names of wives and of loved ones.
Names of places where they come from.

Before they sailed to these fair shores
their old world was the green Azores.
They came across the open seas
these fishermen were Portuguese.

I saw a sign by this old trunk
Ferry Boat to Cuttyhunk.
Within an hour we anchored there
a misty trip in salty air.

When I returned it was time to eat
what would I have as my treat?
A hearty bowl of fishers stew
topped off with a frosty brew.

To end the day I took a stroll
along the streets of cobblestone.
Many shops along the way.
Lovely restaurants by the Bay.

Time has come for me to go
and with this leaving I do know.
Nowhere else can there be found,
the sights and sounds of my hometown.

MANNY

Manny was a regular guy
with a good soul look in his eye.
A handsome man with a friendly smile,
he brightened the day with his charm.

Manny was a man of his word.
A man you could trust.
Someone to be there
when times were tough.

Manny celebrated life.
The ultimate optimist,
he made the best of things;
complain he seldom did.

Manny enjoyed a cold beer and a shot of brandy.
Gardening was his favorite pastime.
On occasion he missed keeping his pigeons.
He won a few races - you know.

Manny loved the Red Sox.
He loved to laugh,
share a silly joke –
and enjoy his many friends.

Manny loved his family most of all,
always happy when they came to call.
He showed kindness and giving
and was very forgiving.

Manny never took the world too serious.
He was a joy to be with.
He was the best.
He was my father.

Playing Catch

In the spring of '59
when all the world seemed fine,
I was just a young boy then –
no more than nine or ten.

Waiting in the front yard
just inside the fence.
I stood there with my ball and glove,
my focus so intense.

Dad would turn the corner
every night at six o'clock.
I'd run up there to meet him
just as he neared the lot.

We played catch and had much fun
throwing the ball around.
He laughed a lot as I ran about -
chasing long fly balls.

Our time was special,
just Dad and me.
We had enough then headed home.
To Mom and suppertime.

The Mohawk Club

My Daddy flew pigeons
when I was a boy;
he and his buddy,
big Eddy McCoy.

He had a coop-
painted it red,
in the back yard.
next to the shed.

His homers were crated
and packed in the truck.
Then off it drove
as he wished them luck.

Five hundred miles
was the length of this race.
A two day drive
to that far away place.

On race day morning
the birds were set free.
Taking to flight –
coming home they would be.

A few days went by –
they appeared in the sky!
A large flock I can see,
Dad shouted with glee.

The droppers were tossed
to decoy them down.
His two birds peeled off
and spiraled towards ground.

They landed real flat
on top of the lat.
Being polled in
they lodged in the trap.

Their bands were removed
and stamped in the clock.
Could Dad have the winner -
the champ of the block?

The race was now over
so the flyers all gathered.
They had silly nick names
that apparently mattered.

There was Shorty, Scotty and Grimba 19,
Ham, Silky, the Barker and Green.
A couple more to round off the score -
like Mr. 45 and his brother 44.

They read all the clocks
and tallied the tapes.
The winner was named
and picked up the stakes.

The purse wasn't large
being generally small.
The thrill of the race
is what summoned them all!

This jolly ol' bunch
were so aptly dubbed -
the pigeon flyers of
the *Mohawk Club*.

This Seafaring Life

Sunrise over the Acushnet.
Across the bay Cuttyhunk rises in the distance.
Trawlers from New Bedford
coming and going from Georges Banks.

In port the auction goes on.
The caller's cadence is music
to men waiting to hear
the price of their catch.

We stayed at the tavern till closing.
Listened to songs of Fado.
Drank to the sea
and the bounty that sustains us.

Recalled times of peril.
How we prayed for help through savage storms.
Remembered our mates who were swallowed by the sea.
Their bodies sank to the graveyard of the deep.

Fishing the sea is in our blood
that is what we know.
We embrace it with our lives.

As sure as there is salt air in our lungs
we accept and respect this ancient profession.
Lord bless our boat and your mighty sea.

Home Again

Ten days out at sea,
mighty swells of forty feet
nearly sank our boat.
We now make port at City Pier.

Today is gray and salty damp.
Off the Bay a cold wind blows.
My collar up to the chin,
shoulders tighten against my scarf.

Old gas lamps light the way.
Slickened streets of cobblestone -
uneven sidewalks made of slate.
All glisten in the evening light.

We make our way to Happy Jacks.
dine upon some homemade soup
with a stuffed quahog or two.
We look around, safe again.
At home in olde New Bedford.

For Market Price

New Bedford fishermen –
olde salts of the sea.
This foggy morning finds them well,
as they listen for the channel bell.

Safe harbor now behind them.
They pass the light on Butlers Flat.
To the fertile grounds off Newfoundland,
Georges Banks and the Flemish Cap.

This trip will bring eight days at sea,
for the gnarly crew of the Gloria B.
At the helm stands a fearless man,
known to all as Captain Dan.

The constant challenge of these waters
brings raging storms on rolling seas,
changing winds with howling gales,
angry skies and freezing rain.

Shifts are worked around the clock.
Sleep will come when the time is right.
In the galley they meet and talk -
while the cook serves up the days delight.

Seines are hung off port and starboard,
dragging bottom or just above.
The boat circles in and endless path,
searching for the pay-day prize.

Two beams bring up the bellowed net,
over the side and straight up top.
The catch is dumped upon the deck,
where rakes are used to sort them out.

In the hold they're packed with ice.
They'll steam for home when the load is full.
When safely docked at harbor side,
they will sell their bounty for Market Price.

The Tree of Joy

It was early Christmas Eve, 1955.
A chilly night – the feel of snow in the air.
I got my wagon out of the shed.
Mom and I set out in search
    of the perfect Christmas tree.

A few blocks away, near the town square,
    was a small lot filled with Christmas trees.
A bearded man, standing by a rusty barrel
    with a flaming fire, pointed out a few.

We spotted this little one
    leaning against a fence
looking sad and lonely.
Hopeless and forlorn.

No one gave it any attention,
would it ever find a home?
We looked at it closely, nice and full
    but decidedly crooked and bent.

Mom said let's buy it,
get it out of the cold.
We loaded the tree on my wagon
    for the short ride home
        to show Dad and little sister.

We had lots of fun with the decorating.
The little tree looked so pretty with
    all the lights and ornaments.
On Christmas morning there were presents
    underneath to keep it company.

That little tree with its crooked bend
brought great joy to our home.
It was indeed a wonderful Christmas.
With the best tree we ever had.

Summer on the Farm

On certain days we baled hay,
then stacked them in the loft.
Hooked them off a flatbed truck,
then placed them on the tram.

Herded cows at 5 o'clock
and moved them towards the barn.
When in their stalls we feed them
while swatting swarming flies.

Rode our bikes to the landing
to swim in the red Slocum river.
Played baseball with our friends –
on the field at Russells Mills.

Camped out on the weekends,
in our tent up on the hill.
Come morning we cooked breakfast,
for us this was a thrill.

We saddled up our horses
and rode the Gooseneck trails;
all the way to Barney's Point
to watch sailboats in the Bay.

As the sun set over the water -
we'd turn and head for home.
We raced along a stretch of beach,
just me and my cousin Dan.

On Labor Day this all would end –
for it was back to school again.
Much fun was had in our childhood days,
spending summer on the farm.

Lawn Talk

Mowing the front lawn
where grass and sidewalk meet.
Connecting with our neighbors
and folks from down the street.

Many walkers are encountered
who say the lawn looks good.
Being complimentary
their remarks are understood.

Engaging them in conversation
they are held captive for awhile.
After gathering my information
I release them with a smile.

Some walk along with dogs
that are sweet and friendly.
Fuss over someone's pet -
they will talk up very kindly.

Sprinkle in some joggers
and a few cyclers too.
You know they never stop.
They'll just wave or nod at you.

The back lawn's very different.
There's not much conversation –
with that backyard gang of critters.
Just entertaining observation.

That Happy Season

Thanksgiving to New Year's,
with Christmas in-between;
there is no happier time of year.
Not even Halloween.

What say you all to merriment,
with lots of food and song.
Come raise a glass of special Grog.
Join in and sing along.

Gather 'round the olde fireplace.
With friends and family.
Pet the dog and pat the cat.
Light up your Christmas tree.

Unwrap a gift and give one too.
That's what we like to do.
Remember this is Christmas time.
And a Merry one to you!!

Where the House Once Stood

The wrecking ball came today
crashing through the roof,
destroying all that stood.
The old house collapsed;
reduced to a pile of rubble.

Looking close,
I can see myself in every room.
Scenes from earlier times
played in my head.

The remains carted away –
walls, doors, bricks and boards.
In a wind swept cloud of dust,
the soul of the house drifted skyward.

Seasons come and go.
Winter snows and summer suns.
But memories never vanish;
they remain, asleep in the
rooms of my mind.

Long after passing years,
the ball field grass still grows
over familiar ground
where the house once stood.

Surviving Catholic School

There I was in Kindergarten.
My Mom brought me there
then turned and walked away.
My journey had begun
at Saint John the Baptist School.

I should have been excited
but that I could not be.
Look at all those nuns
then tell me what you see.
This was no jolly group
it wasn't fun for me.

Do penguins stand that tall?
Such odd looking creatures
for they had no ears at all.
Shrouded in black they stood
with their face under a hood.

A large white bib
covered their chest.
Were they sloppy eaters?
Who wears a bib all day?

Two things I won't forget.
The infamous Baltimore Catechism
and that boring Palmer Method -
those pens and messy ink-wells.

I recall the second grade nun -
meanest of the mean.
She made you slap yourself.
We were all so helpless then.

Many kids scared to death
wet themselves from fear.
The janitor dropped sawdust –
to absorb the puddled floor.

Our principal was a brute.
She was also the eighth grade nun.
Always yelling and smacking heads
that's what she liked to do.

They were masters of humiliation.
At the blackboard –
never struggle with a math problem.
Their verbal abuse would tear you apart,
reduce you to tears.

Those nuns of yesteryear
would be in jail today.
Doing time, ten to twenty
for child abuse.

They were a miserable bunch.
Those Religious Sisters of Mercy.
They may have been religious –
but they knew no mercy.

Twenty seven survived,
all the way from K through 8.
We made the journey.
It was 1962 - our time to graduate!

Hello to the 27: Bobby, Donna, Susan F, Kenny, Mary-Anne, Anthony,
Sheila C, Kathy, James, Susan D, Robert, JoAnne, Peter, Mary-Lou,
Danny, Suzanne, George, Claire, Jerry, Billy, Ray, Debbie, Paul, Jimmy,
Joe, Sheila H, David.

Tornado Time

It was July hot in Texas.
When a mighty wind did roar.
The night was loud with thunder
when hell knocked at our door.

Lightning bolts lit up the sky.
The hail ripped up the roof.
Things were flying all around
making such an awful sound.

Warning sirens began to blare.
Giving us a frightful scare.
Windows shattered with a blast.
It all happened very fast.

Our bodies shook from fear.
Could the end of us be near?
We huddled with our cats and dogs
inside the bathroom square.

Struggling with our thoughts
we said a family prayer.
Oh Lord, lead us out of Austin.
And take us home to Boston.

The Road to Wimberley

You ride the devil's backbone, the ridge above the valley.
Through rolling Hill-Country, among the cedar trees.
Along the Rio Blanco to the town of Wimberley.
Her streets are wide and dusty, her buildings old and plain.
Take a walk down Kirby Lane, with its shops and restaurants.
Observe the hitching rails; you may see a horse near by.

Step upon the sidewalks of splintered wooden planks.
Stroll Olde Town Plaza, built with wood and limestone.
Visit Christmas Place, buy a handmade trinket.
Spend time with Ule. She owns the Wild West Store.
Buy yourself some boots and enjoy a tale or two.
Say hi to her dog Rusty, he'll greet you at the door.

At the Prickly Pear Café or Miss Mae's Bar-B-Q.
Make time for lunch, enjoy the Southwest flavor.
Try Burger Barn home of "Dang Good Vittles."
Such a lovely town, filled with special things.
There is much to see and do, so take your time today.
Just thirty miles from Austin. Turn south at Dripping Springs.

Retirement II

Time has come for me to go.
There is nothing more to tell.
So I'll take their EPO.
All that ends is well.

My career has ended now.
Like the Cowboy in the movie
I'll ride into tomorrow.
Take my memories with me.

I'll sleep late in the morning.
Wake up to birds singing.
Take breakfast on the patio,
with many cups of coffee.

More time with my sweet wife.
Play with my dog Annie.
Take trips around New England.
Write myself some poems.

My world is different now.
These times they are so special.
Each morning is a blessing.
Each day is to be lived.

Old Buddies

The years are all but gone,
but old buddies continue on.

Every day they see the sun,
and have themselves some fun.

They sit around and reminisce,
of things they did and things they missed.

In their prime and being bold,
chased the ladies or so I'm told.

With fancy cars and pick-up lines,
they met in bars and so opined.

They talk of sports and politics,
of family matters and their grandkids.

Today's headlines are on their minds.
How life has changed in their time.

Most of all they seem content,
to talk of days and what they meant.

They raise a glass of favorite brew,
because that is what old buddies do.

Our Adobe Home

We had a home in Texas,
down by the cedar trees.
Nestled in the Hill Country,
near the Colorado River.
Austin was our new home.
The adventure had begun.

The neighborhood was varied,
a very eclectic bunch.
Across the road lived Aggie –
the man from College Station.
On our left were Shulpa and G2.
Big George lived to our right.

There was crazy Virginia
and Jim with his guns.
Andrew and Tammy,
John and Luanne.
Al Lopez and Inca his wife.
These were our neighbors,
all part of our life.

We sat on the front porch,
kicked back with our margaritas.
Looking up at the red Texas sky.
We marveled at the evening sunsets.
Pretty hummingbirds hovered –
sipping nectar from our flowers.
Mule deer helped themselves –
feasting on front yard plants.

We managed the oppressive heat
and those wild tornado nights.
We had snakes in the garden
and scorpions in the garage.
Turkey vultures flew around,
searching for prey on the ground.
Grackles chirped their screeching sound
and armadillos were seldom found.

A charming home, warm and cozy
with tiled floors in amber tones.
A living room with a grand fireplace -
ablaze in late evening hours.
Walls adorned with style.
A well appointed house indeed.

Diane's stained glass work
hung artistically in cathedral windows.
Colors permeated the rooms with an aura.
Sun passing through each crafted piece.
I decorated the garage - sports stuff.
My old ball gloves and all things Boston.

A whole decade had now come to pass -
our time in the southwest was closing.
Soon we'd be back in New England.
In the end we would understand,
we weren't really cut out for Texas,
but we did love our adobe home.

Coming Home

Twenty years have passed
since I saw my father's house.
Leaving there a young man
for adventure on the sea.
I signed onboard a merchant ship
to sail the world for free.

The excitement was amazing
in all those ports of call.
Many cultures I encountered.
Some strange and quite bizarre.
Many ladies I spent time with-
shared their hearts with me.

Educated by the world -
little time was spent in school.
My days at sea are closing fast.
I am weathered from the storms.
The final port awaits me -
I am coming home.

IV
ABOUT
PETS

About Pets

How precious they are, our little pets.
Greeting us each morning with their waging tails.

Saying hi with their happy smiles and cheerful barks
when we come home at the end of the day.

They are part of our family,
woven into our lives.

We must show them much love
and shower them with praise.

Keep them close to our hearts and enjoy them.
They are here with us for just a little while.

Dear Smokey

You were our special little cat.
Always there with your happy self.
You gave us lots of love -
hours of endless joy.
You were a comfort to us all.

We couldn't wait
to hold you close.
To see your tiny face
and kiss your furry head.

You made us laugh a lot –
with your antics and your ways.
You were such a little clown
the way you jumped around.

So sad the day has come,
when now your time is done.
The emptiness we feel,
will take some time to heal.
Our mourning time will pass,
then once again we'll laugh.

Your spirit will endure,
and your song again we'll sing.
Forever in our hearts,
your memory will rest.
In a distant day -
we will meet again and play.

Good bye our Smokey Boy.

Mornings with Nugget

I hear the birds this morning
outside my bedroom window –
chirping their daily reveille.

Getting up, I whistle for the Boy.
He waits by the bathroom
while I throw water on my face.

We go downstairs to greet the day
and prepare for our morning walk.
He is his usual excited self.

It is a marvelous fall day.
He enjoys sniffing at the crisp air,
there is a brisk snap to his pace.

Around the neighborhood, we stroll.
He chases every squirrel he sees and
barks at any dog that comes our way.

This little guy is king of the walk,
the proudest Chihuahua you ever saw.
Nine pounds of pure love and fun.

We stop by Cedar Park Pond
and feed some bread to the Geese.
Their hissing sound drives him back.

Having come full circle -
we are back at the house.
It is time for breakfast.

I give Nugget his usual dish.
That always makes him happy.
Eating is his favorite thing.

I sit down with the daily paper
and read the headlines to him.
He turns around and looks up at me.

After having my cup of coffee
it is time for me to go to work.
I love my mornings with Nugget.

Ridin with My Dog

On weekends we go ridin
in my yellow pick-up truck.
Along Flatbone Ridge,
through rolling Hill Country.

Nugget on my lap
his head resting on my arm.
He looks out the window,
it's Saturday again.

We tune in Country 93.
I sing the songs I know.
We kick up backroad dust,
all the way from Cedar Park to Fredericksburg.

We stop for breakfast
in the town of Marble Falls.
The *Bluebonnet Café*
has become our favorite spot.

We eat out in the back
on a wooden picnic table.
I have my coffee black
we share some scrambled eggs.

Soon we finish up,
stretch our legs a bit.
Get back in the truck
to continue with our day.

My Horse, My Dog and Me

The wind is harsh
blowing strong –
across the desert floor.
Sand biting at my face.
I cannot close a door.

This old road goes on forever.
There is no end in sight.
We look up at the velvet sky.
The moon is full tonight.

With many miles still to go –
before we reach our town.
We pull up near a mound of rocks
and here we settle down.

We make a fire to keep us warm
and camp out by a tree.
It is just the three of us.
My horse, my dog and me.

V
SPORTS
and
MUSIC

Forever Fenway

Our ballpark on Yawkey Way will be 100 this April.
Ghosts of seasons past will come to life.
Great moments re-visited, memories will abound.
Players who patrolled the green outfield pastures
and danced on the dirt paths of the infield,
will be remembered in the era of their play.

My special memory is the team of 1967.
We called them the Impossible Dream,
with names like Yaz, Rico, Boomer, Lonborg and Tony C.
We had our darkest day when Jack's fastball took Tony down.
Regrouping from that loss we enjoyed the splendor of that summer,
wining the Pennant on the last day of the season.

This team changed the culture of the organization –
the re-invention of the Red Sox began and the Nation was born.
Evolving from losers to winners they raised the standard of achievement.
They will live forever in the hearts of New Englanders.
Three cheers for the BOSOX and the hallowed ground of Fenway.
Let *Sweet Caroline* and *Shipping up to Boston* be sung at every game.
May the flag always fly over centerfield and the Green Monstah stand
forever.

Another Spring

Falling softly on the grass
the earthy smell of rain
hangs in the morning air.
A delightful scene before us.

We look out at our garden
and say hello to little buds.
Many flowers will appear
in their splendid colors.

Looking at the trees
leaves are filling in.
Birds begin to sing
and squirrels run about.

To protect the garden veggies,
a scarecrow plays his role.
Those silly little rabbits
will feast on everything.

A lovely time of year.
A time for new beginnings
when we can start again.
Hope and opportunity
bring in another spring.

The Boys of Fenway

They came to play
    and spank the Yanks.
These Sox of Red
    were far from dead.

So they polished their bats
    and sharpened their cleats.
Who are these Yanks?
    Can't they be beat?

The Sox had won none,
    so the Yanks had the fun,
they roared in their glee
    having won the first three.

Now we needed all four
    lest we are swept off the floor -
and they needed one more
    before closing the door.

So we buckled right down
    in that fancy big town –
we took the next three
    and then the last one.

The Pennant is ours!
    Our job was well done.
It was 2004 –
    we'd be second no more.
T'was a lot of joy shared
    on that chilly fall day.
As the Pennant was raised
    over dear old Fenway.

The Pitching Ace

In the center of the diamond
stands a lonely baseball man.
A pitcher by his trade –
alone with ball in hand,
atop the pitcher's mound,
where everything begins.

A pitcher gets a sign
from his catcher down below.
He does this every time
on each successive throw.
Like an artist with a brush
the craftsman paints the plate.

The target is presented –
location is the key.
He mixes in a fast ball,
that curves above the knee.
This is an age old art
mastered only by a few.

He delivers with a motion
poised in balance and precision.
Commander of the zone –
controlling every game.
He is the pitching Ace –
the stopper of the staff.

Another Season

Her seats are empty now,
covered in December snow.
Fenway in winter,
just getting through the cold.

Yawkey Way is quiet.
Parking lots are vacant.
Street vendors missing.
No balls off the Monstah.

We anticipate the coming season.
Those hawkers in the stands
selling peanuts, hot dogs
and ice cold beer.

Our outfield will be strong,
the infield has the range.
Our pitching staff is solid
and we have speed to steal bases.

Can we beat those Yanks -
win our Division?
Enjoy another World Series
in the October sun?

The love of the game remains.
Baseball – the greatest of them all.
God bless the RED SOX.
See you in Boston.

Blues Man

Up from Memphis,
singing the blues.
A straw hat on his head
and pearly white shoes.

Picking a guitar
in a style of his own.
He sings from the soul
with a gentle-like moan.

He plays for the basket
this Saturday night.
The crowd is good.
And the mood just rite.

Gladiators of the Circled Square

In their corners stood the boxers;
waiting for the bell.
The match was set for fifteen rounds,
a short time spent in hell.

Caution ruled the early rounds -
as they scoped each other out.
Throwing only jabs –
they circled all about.

Middle rounds took their toll
from the pounding given out.
The outcome at this point
was very much in doubt.

Lefts, rights and uppercuts –
followed them around.
Clutched against the ropes,
a head butt made a sound.

Their bodies told the story,
of the savagery released.
This was no night for glory,
from a fight that was the beast.

Their eyes cut and swollen.
Their noses bent and twisted.
Crimson streaks crossed their face
a sight not for the timid.

The ferocity was brutal,
fatigue had now set in.
Their legs no longer steady –
no towel was thrown in.

In the twelfth a fighter fell
from a smashing heavy blow.
A final punch was thrown
that would truly end the show.

His head bounced on the canvas.
His eyes stared out in space.
A knockout was recorded.
The time was stamped in place.

Riding for the Prize

Sit down beside me;
listen to my song.
About my bygone days
and how I got along.

It was '65 in Houston,
I headed for the road –
in my old truck, with that
leather bag and saddle.

My bill fold had some money
just enough to reach Cheyenne.
My draw was not so good,
I didn't make that ride.

I placed well in Reno,
hurt my arm a bit.
Good prize money –
helped to ease the pain.

A few days rest was needed
before I saw Las Vegas.
The national finals –
must be at my best.

For years that was my life,
long lonesome roads and
sad old country songs.
Nights in cheap hotels
needing lovers more than friends.

Cowboys love the Rodeo,
their boots, hats and lariats.
From San Antone to Calgary
we all chased the prize.

Sit down beside me;
listen to my song.
About my bygone days
and how I got along.

Redd Lane

A full arena, many fans had come out,
an anxious mood as you looked about.
An angry sky threatened the play.
Could this be an omen to ruin the day?

It was rodeo time, July in Cheyenne.
Many a Cowboy would try their hand.
Saddle Bronc Riders opened the show.
Skilled Team Ropers were next to go.

Bull Riding – the event of the day.
Top prize of the PRCA.
One by one they entered the chutes,
to give it a go and spur with their boots.

Up came the leader Redd Lane
over the fence to mount his ride.
A big grey bull - they called High Tide.

The cheering crowd grew very loud.
Stomping their feet clapping their hands –
noise echoing throughout the stands

Off went the gun as they opened the gate –
the snorting beast reared twisting through "8".
Again the gun sounded ending his ride.
As Redd dismounted he was struck in the side,
by a horn from the Tide who had turned.

A crushing blow knocked Redd down,
curled in the mud he lay by the clown.
The crowd rose to their feet, silent and stunned,
their rodeo champion fallen and done.

His heart pierced from a broken rib.
The wagon rolled in to take him away.
All stood in the rain feeling his pain.
The last ride for Cowboy Redd Lane.

Singing Bird Café

Left my home one summer day
    filled with hope, desire and grit.
Rode a Greyhound out of Boston
    down to Nashville, Tennessee.

All I brought was my guitar
    and a pocket full of songs.
Took a chance and made this move
    to chase my master dream.

Got myself a room to rent
    in a rundown boarding house.
Walked the downtown streets each day
    looking for a job.

Came upon a window sign -
    Help Wanted inquire within.
They hired me on the spot
    at the Singing Bird Café.

I was now a waiter –
    serving burgers, fries and beer.
On my first night the evening act
    showed up stinking drunk.
I asked if I could fill in -
    and sing my songs for free.

The frantic owner said to me -
    Go show us what you got.
I walked on stage with my guitar
    and sat there on that stool.

Picked some songs that I wrote
    and sang them for the crowd.
When I wrapped up they cheered for me
    with a warm and long applause.
That was my beginning –
    The next night I got paid.

Whiskey Nights

Morning finds me alone
in the back seat of my car.
Not sure how I got here –
too much whiskey from last night.

I roll down the window
 feel the air against my face.
Shake my head,
to clear the numbness from my mind.

Blinded by the early sun
my eyes need some help.
I fumble for my shades,
climb into the front seat
and head straight for home.

Entering through the front door
I stumble up the stairs,
flop into bed
and fall asleep for hours.

Old dreams run through my head
of what I let pass by.
The next morning I recover
from my evening episode.

I pull on my boots
my old blue jeans and hat.
I step outside.
The sounds of morning greet me.

Seeing my refection in a window
I tell myself
the time is now -
make happen,
those faded dreams of yesterday.

Guitar Man

The road is long and lonely,
away from home so long.
The band becomes my family,
the bus becomes our home.

I make music with my guitar,
sing songs that I write.
On stage in Honky Tonks,
to a full house on Saturday night.

Our eight week tour nearly over;
as we move on to San Antone.
We'll wind up at the Copeland,
pack up and head for home.

We found our way to some success
thanks to all our fans.
I've seen the country coast to coast,
made friends along the way.

A country singing Guitar Man.
Is all I want to be.
This minstrel life is all I've known.
It's sure been good to me.

Over Again

Memphis saw me wasted.
With a ticket for New Orleans,
to play my horn again.
Passed out in the station,
toked out on the weed,
waiting for the 'Hound.

For a time I had it all.
I walked in high cotton.
But that's all over now.
There are no more victories.
There are no more songs.

I have won and I have lost,
but I always came to play.
I never ran the clock out.
I played it to the end.

Mostly I'm confused.
I do not understand.
What I had is gone.
It is time to reassess.

I need someone to hold.
Perhaps to settle down.
My emotions run away.
I just hear the thunder and feel the rain.
The rainbow vanished from the sky.
I am out of love and left behind.

Alone at the end of the day.
The lights are all turned off.
And the seats are all empty.
I come back on stage
to look at the arena.
And play it over again.

Lucky Jack

A gambling man I know
does play a game or two.
He plays downtown –
and all around -
in clubs and living rooms.

Enjoys his gin and tonic,
and likes to play Black Jack.
But Poker is his natural game,
cards to him are all the same.

He dabbles in Gin Rummy too,
and plays that game on-line
with players that he does not know.
To him that is just fine.

He flies out to Las Vegas
to taste the big time game.
When up against the best
he fares with some success.

At times, he plays the ponies
at the track and OTB.
But he never bets the Greyhounds.
The rabbit has left town.

Rubs elbows with some bookies,
to bet on sporting games.
To him that is too costly -
the vig he feels is lame.

Casinos are his second home.
To the poker tables he does roam.
At Foxwoods in the mornings,
and the Sun in afternoons.

He loves the gambling life
so he never took a wife.
Now retired and laid back.
The gambling world remembers,
the man called Lucky Jack.

Jukebox

In the corner there's a Jukebox
inside of old Gruene Hall.
Waiting there patiently
up against the wall.

Some good ole boys come on by
and drop their quarters in.
For the chance to hear some songs
from Willie, Kris and Jim.

In the corner there's a Jukebox
loaded up with songs.
Some are just for dancin
and some for sing along.

Songs that take us back in time
to how things used to be.
Sometimes you need a song
to make a memory.

That Jukebox in the corner
up against the wall -
the featured main attraction
standing proud and tall.

They'll be back next Friday night,
the girls and all the boys.
To pick up where they left off
and listen to the noise.

VI
THE
STRUGGLE

Beyond the Wooded Edge

I walked into the woods today
alone but not afraid.
Trees were full of leaves
not yet in Autumn turn.
I found a worn out path
and followed it along.
It took me by a stream
where rippling waters flow
then curved around a pond
with ducks and geese at play.

I found myself a rock
where I could sit and think.
No human sounds were heard
no voices or machines.
All that I could hear
was the sound of nature's song.
This was a pleasant walk.
In the splendor of it all,
there is another world
beyond the wooded edge.

Finding My Way

Standing at the top of the stairs
I hear the noise.
I feel the vast emptiness -
the loss of all that could have been and never was.

What are the reasons?
There are no explanations.
So many questions.
Where are the answers?
I am overwhelmed.

There is no denying the sadness I feel
as darkness rolls in around me.
I look for tomorrow when peace will prevail.
Hoping I find the light and my way to happiness,
where at the end of the road all will be forgiven.

I believe love fuels our will to survive -
being the healer that allows us
to fall into favor with our past.
Giving us space to search
for that special moment,
that defines who we are.

Across the Border

Midnight falls on Front Street.
Heavy fog rolls off the Hudson.
Danger floats in the air.
Blue guardians walk their beat.

In the bowels of the city
steady traffic moves along.
Money passes hands
in the dim light of the moon.

Nothing here but winos,
ladies dressed in red,
addicts, old drunks,
thieves and indigents.

People of the street
a gathering of unfortunates.
Hopeless and forlorn.
All wards of the universe.

Many stories linger here
of a long fall from grace.
Dark clouds cover their sun
denying them any warmth.

Lost souls in a wide abyss
searching for a sign.
Looking for the border.
Will they ever make it home?

A Day in the Journey

Alone I walk through the Garden.
A gentle peace surrounds me,
offering comfort, a shield from hurt.
Here, I am no longer in harm's way.

I find clarity and sense of purpose.
I see where I have been.
My destination true.
I move forward on my journey.

Along the way I see faces in time
peering at me through little windows.
Their expressions touch me,
each with their own message.

As I near the end of this day,
I truly understand –
That love is what matters
and life is for now.

This Mornings Walk

I walk along the beach.
The morning air is crisp.
No crowds in early March.
Solitude is calming.
Pounding surf a symphony.
Nature – soothing to the soul.

I watch little birds scampering
near the waters edge.
Carefree winged companions
entertain me with their antics.

The recent past is troubling me.
Unable to forget what happened.
I struggle with the vision
embedded in my mind.
I must find the strength to let it go.
This morning's walk will help.

Use My Shoulder

How can I comfort you –
in your hour of stress?
Is there something I can do
to straighten out the mess?

Why do you worry so,
can things be all that bad?
When I look at you –
your eyes seem very sad.

Rest your troubles on my shoulder,
stop here for a while.
Feel comfort in my arms –
and let me see your smile.

State of Mind

Trapped in the maze of life.
Lost without direction.
Confused beyond belief.
The struggle has no end.

The sky is gray and black.
The rain will not let up.
Depression takes its grasp.
Eating at my soul.

Will tomorrow be the same,
an endless sad refrain?
Will I ever laugh again?
Will a smile ever grace my face?

There has to be an end.
This state cannot continue.
When morning arrives.
I hope to see the sun.

The Road

The sun is down, nighttime is upon us.
The sky is clear, the dessert cold.
Tequila helps ease the chill.
You lying beside me adds more warmth.

We're a long way from home.
Before us the road of uncertainty,
bound to have many turns.
With luck we'll make the right ones.

No matter how far we roam
or how difficult times may be,
love and faith will guide us.
In the end we know –
we'll always roll back home again.

Triumph and Success

At the moment I remain
overwhelmed from the burden.
Soon I will be free and stronger
for what I am going through.

I will be wiser from the experience
and ready for what comes next.
I am mostly alone in this matter.
With little help from anyone.

I am under the gun
with mounting pressure.
In the end they can all go to hell.
I will triumph and success will be my reward.

The Effect of Love and Evil

Love sparks a fire
filled with passion and desire.
Evil dulls the soul
in the end it takes a toll.

Make room for the Lovers
there are too few of them.
Keep hope for the Sinners
so they can be redeemed.

Do Lovers have the power
or do Sinners have the edge?
The strong will learn to love
while the weak fall into sin.

Fan the fire of love -
you shall feel the warmth.
Douse the flames of evil
before they burn the day.

Unburdened

Long is the road before me.
Far and wide the distance.
Born from the ashes of despair.
Now fueled by hope and desire.
I reach up to touch the sky.

No longer burdened by guilt.
From the weight suppressing my soul.
Unshackled from this bondage.
The mind and spirit are free.
And the air is fresh and clear.

The road to freedom begins.
A path will soon unfold.
The future will be mine.
For I can see tomorrow.
This life is to be lived.

Today

Fear not the days ahead
they are not yet known to us.
Our yesterdays are gone.
We have learned from what has past.

There are no secrets now –
no clues to figure out.
What we see is real.
It's where we are today.

The Eagle and the Rat

I felt cold from the rain.
The sun offered no warmth.
The stars never twinkled.
And the moon never shined.

The neighborhood was sad,
decayed and rundown.
Depression weighed heavily,
I was always looking down.

The feel of my surroundings
left emptiness inside me.
I felt I was damaged
like the things I saw around me.

Would the ghetto claim my soul?
Would I survive to pay the toll?

Twenty years did pass,
when I left at last.
To shed the awful stain,
to rid myself of pain.

My struggle with the demon
finally reached an end.
The place I now move to
would be my newest friend.

How wonderful this freedom
from the shackles of the slum.
I could now look back
and see how far I'd come.

My home was now near Rockdale,
    by the park at Buttonwood.
Our new neighbor was a lawyer -
    no more roughnecks from the hood.

I had a new beginning and new identity.
    My fortunes now were changing
    with the energy I found.
All I had to do was take a look around.

How grand this was to happen
    to a son of Second Street.
How nice it was to find myself
    in a place that was so sweet.

The raucous days were over,
    no more rumblings in the street.
Now I fly with the Eagle.
No more days with the Rat.

Beyond the Sky

Grieving has passed.
Mourning time is over.
I have no more tears.
My memory of a shared life
everlasting as the universe.
Forever you walk with me.

When I call your name -
I hear you in the sound of the waves.
I feel you in the warmth of the sun.
I see you in the reflection of the moon.
Someday I will hold you again,
behind that door - beyond the sky.

Say Good-Bye

Lost and alone.
I walk these empty city streets.
No one is around
to hear me make a sound.
The only friend I have today
is my shadow on the ground.

Sitting on a park bench,
I look towards the sky.
The morning sun shines on my face,
bringing me warmth.

Looking into your eyes
I cannot find you there.
Your heart no longer loves.
There is nothing I can change.
I have done all that I can do.
I have wallowed in my tears.

No longer will I sit and cry
wasting time wondering why.
Having fought the aging madness.
The time has come to say good-bye.

Sixty-Five

Visions wander back and forth
   within my conscious mind.
Familiar scenes from yesteryear –
   are pictured all so clear.
Sounds of youthful voices –
   echo in the wind.

Things I once did with ease
   no longer done so well.
The energy of long ago –
   left on the field of play.
Youthful times have come and gone
   with tides upon the shore.

As age goes fine with wine and cheese
   so too does age go well with me.
I am at peace with all that's past
   and happy where I am.
I feel today very much alive.
   Life is grand at sixty-five!

All Things Matter Now

These days we spend together
become the memories of tomorrow.
I love each one of them.
Long weekend country drives.
Early morning walks –
with conversations in the park.

Look up at the evening sky –
see the overture of light.
The stars how they do twinkle
and sparkle oh so bright.

I take your hand in mine
in the soft glow of the moon.
I hold you close to me
and whisper in your ear –
sweet things of love my dear.

In the many years to come –
when you reach out to me
I will ask what I can do.
This I promise you -
because all things matter now.

Added Years

Will you walk beside me –
to be there should I fall.
Years are adding up.
I stand no longer tall.

While our steps begin to slow.
Our spirit stays alive.
That smile upon your face
makes everything worthwhile.

Now, our friends are few.
Many took the train
to that place beyond the stars –
but you my dear remain
so close and ever near.

I try to believe in forever
but forever just lasts so long.
I struggle with the fear
of never seeing you again.

I pray for tomorrow,
to see your lovely face,
hear your sweet voice
and feel your warm embrace.

Reflecting on our memories,
letting go of faded dreams.
The many years we had –
our heaven here on earth.

Journey's End

When my days are over
with the end drawing near.
Will you look upon me kindly
for the years I was here.

What did I accomplish
within my span of time.
Was I a good man
to the folks I left behind.

Take me home to rest
in that graveyard by the sea.
Near the chapel at Saint Johns,
where the bells will ring for me.

Do not send me flowers
nor shed yourself a tear –
gather round my old friends
and celebrate with cheer.

Sing my favorite song
then lower me in the ground –
cover me with good earth,
no more to make a sound.

As I say my last good-bye,
I would be so glad –
if you smiled upon the memory,
of those yesterdays we had.

VII
WORLD
ORDER

The Visit

Who knocks at my door today?
   I invite the stranger in.
I offer drink and warmth.
   He tells me of his journey,
and the message that he brings.

He speaks of love and kindness
   and a peace that is to come.
He says that we should pray,
   for the family of the world.

I ask him for his name.
   He replies that he's an angel
and has chosen me this day.
   He looks at me and smiles,
then turns and walks away.

Harmony and Brotherhood

Hear that bluebird at my window,
sing a pretty song for me.
Lying in bed I wonder
how will I face the day.

The world we use to live in
twisted and damaged.
Political correctness
has sent us down the road to hell.

Terrorists scourging the world order.
Be they foreign or domestic
they are devils, a bleeding sore
on the soul of humanity.
I curse them, their ideology
and everything they stand for.

I went to church today –
not sure why.
Just felt the need to go.
I had no rosary to pray
or holy book to read.
I followed the service
and wallowed in the words.

Was I a better person when I left?
Probably not –
but I did feel special.
That feeling carried me through the day.
I prayed for universal harmony
and the brotherhood of mankind.

This Belongs to US

The French have their Ballet.
England claims the Theatre.
Italians own the Opera.
Americans – we have the Western.

Television gave us heroes -
Hoppy, Gene and Roy.
Atop their gallant steeds -
Topper, Champion and Trigger.

Movies have their heroes too,
The Duke, Clint, Duval and Cooper.
All lead characters
good guys with their unique style.

We have classic Westerns -
High Noon, True Grit, Unforgiven.
Legendary characters –
Ringo Kid, Hondo and Shane.

We have Cowboys and Gunfighters.
Stetson hats and bandannas.
A Winchester rifle and six-shooter,
everyday tools of survival.

Old dusty prairie towns   -
with a general store, jail and livery.
Always a saloon, piano man,
dance hall girls and card playing dudes.

We can't forget the lawmen –
Sheriff, Marshal or Deputy.
Displaying their silver badge,
protecting town folk from bad guys.

Westerns depict a code of honor,
respect, justice and loyalty.
A unique American art form,
belonging only to US.

The Last Chief

So long ago we lingered there,
inside the canyon walls.
Our order never came
the sign to guide us all.

We made our camp at sunset
with a fire to keep us warm.
The howl of the coyote –
was our evening serenade.

The walls of the adobe,
sheltered us at night.
Inside the Palo Duro –
the moon so full and bright.

In pursuit of Quanah –
we stepped upon their land.
Inside the tribal lodge –
Mackenzie gave his hand.

With the leader of his nation –
they smoked the pipe of peace.
A final tribute to the warrior –
the last Comanche chief.

Three Days in July

A northern wind comes blowing in –
sweeping cannon smoke away.
Soldiers clad in blue and gray –
lay scattered all about.

Looking out across a field –
guns are silent on the ridge.
The Southern cause defeated,
the Union has prevailed.

Meade and Lee fought here for three.
Soon Abe will come to speak
on this hallowed earth made red with blood.
The battle sound forever heard
still echoes here in Gettysburg.

Up from Laredo

April arrived –
another cattle drive north.
Cowboys and Wranglers
gather along the Rio Grande.

A sweet fragrance of spring grass permeates the prairie air.
Longhorns and strays rounded up
and mixed with ranchers stock.

A heard of 3,000 begins moving -
slowly towards San Antone
en route to Fort Worth,
crossing the Red River.

Oklahoma Indian lands –
give rise to cautious awareness.
Trading skills will be helpful in providing safe passage.

The overland drive will take two months
before reaching Kansas City's railheads.
We'll sleep on the ground with a bedroll
and a saddle for a pillow.

Cowboys love their horses,
sharing a bond of survival.
Each drive provides adventure,
the freedom and beauty of the open range.

Trail drives are long, comforts are few.
Many days in the wind, rain and sun.
Meals come off the wagon,
evening campfires provide solace.

Stopping for supplies in trail towns,
provides free time.
Saloons swell with patrons,
thirsty for whiskey and beer.

At the end of the line
the stock are sold off,
shipped via rail to big cities in the east.
Everyone draws their pay.

We all linger awhile.
Most would soon head back home.
Next spring, another long drive
will bring us up from Laredo.

The Charge

In July of '63.
Three days before the 4th.
Two armies crossed paths.

The peaceful village of Gettysburg
would never be the same.
The state of a nation divided
was about to go insane.

Forces led by Lee and Meade,
would clash for three straight days.
It was to be a costly struggle,
between the Blues and the Grays.

Just beyond the field of battle
Federals assembled on the high ridge.
Rebels lined up in the woods.

Confederates launched a cannonade.
Having no affect on the Union position,
their effort fell in vain.

When the cannon fire stopped
southerners stepped from the woods.
Moved across a wide open field,
charging the center of the Federal line.

Confederate soldiers drew closer,
Union troops could hear their Rebel Yell.
Yankee muskets unleashed a wall of fire
devastating the oncoming infantry.

Pickett's Division was no more.
They would regroup and retreat
forming their now shortened columns.
They marched back home in defeat.

The War Between the States raged on.
The struggle would end at Appomattox,
Lee would surrender to Grant.
National scars would remain forever.

Feather and the Bull

(1890)

On the great plains of the Dakotas
in the nation of the Sioux –
stood two Lakota people –
Snow Feather and Dancing Bull.

On the Pine Ridge Reservation
in the light of an August moon,
Spotted Elk the elder Chief –
joined their hands as one.

Villagers filled the lodge
for the ceremony of love.
Simple gifts were brought.
Hides and potted beads.

By the days of early winter
their happiness short lived.
The 7TH Cavalry arrived
with their Hotchkiss mountain guns.

They laid waste to everything.
The village overwhelmed.
A massacre of the innocent.
So many blood stains in the snow.

A trooper took down the Bull.
Feather survived the slaughter.
Her broken heart aching.
The Great-Spirit called her home.

A Child of War

She rose up from the ashes,
the rubble and the squalor.
Her village lay in ruin
as the army marches out.
A little girl in tattered clothes
calls out to a soldier.

Please wait -
do not leave me here.
I am cold and hungry
and have no shoes to wear.
Please take me with you -
I have no home to go to.

With unknown roads ahead
she cannot walk alone.
Her family is no longer.
Tyranny claimed their souls.
A soldier picks her up
and leaves her at a church.

Changed in Time

Shots rang out in Dallas.
On the streets of Dealey Plaza.
JFK was blown away.
In the fall of '63.

'68 would come too soon.
Shooters struck again.
April's bullet toppled Martin,
then Bobby fell in June.

Our country was in turmoil
from the war in Vietnam.
Hey Hey LBJ - how many kids did you kill today?

Riots broke out in our cities.
Streets became combat zones.
Hoses opened wide on citizens,
pushing them back against the wall.

Violence boiled in the south.
Freedom riders disappeared.
Churches burned in Birmingham.
Criminal acts of the hooded Klan.

Looking toward the future,
we dreamed of love and peace.
Our youth was filled with hope,
that we would make a difference.

We had our share of sit-ins -
smoked grass to mellow-out.
We stood up to the police,
when they pushed us all about

Wearing flowers in our hair
we marched in bannered groups –
locked arm in arm for safety,
singing common protest songs.

We stood strong together.
Fought for causes that were real
civil rights and woman's rights,
and all that was unjust.

Reached out to help the poor.
Joined in to feed the hungry.
Burned our bras and draft cards too.
Prayed for peace throughout the world.

From '61 to '69 –
those years were not so kind.
In nearly half a century –
how much has changed in time?

Desperate to be Heard

Home from Vietnam.
A wounded young man,
confused and rejected
walks the streets alone.

Haunted by memories
and visions in his head.
He cannot purge his mind
of the horrors he has seen.

Sadness covers his heart.
A tormented empty soul –
shrouded in pain
exposed to the bone.

Desperate to be heard
who will hear his cry?
You can't talk to people
who don't want to listen.

No one really cares.
THEY DON'T WANT TO KNOW!
Indifference, disrespect and fear
so difficult to deal with.

One night he got drunk
the next night he got stoned.
Then he pulled himself together -
and got up off the floor.

He thought of his old girlfriend
then called on sweet Elaine.
She opened up her arms
and embraced him with a smile.

That Friday Morning

Shameful news was heard today.
Of little children blown away.
Unstable minds do unspeakable things.
Vicious evil the gunman brings.

He had a mother, a father too.
What was it they failed to do?
He practiced at a firing range.
With his mother, oh so strange.

Access to guns must be curtailed.
Damaged minds must be detailed.
And where are you; the NRA.
What is it that you have to say.

The gun lobby is very strong.
And politicians know it's wrong.
But they take the money anyway.
The innocent are left to pay.

The tragedy of Sandy Hook.
Remembered for the lives it took.
We mourn those lives lost that day.
Let's pray that evil stays away.

Bobby Gainz

Graduating from High School –
in the spring of '66.
We took different roads.
I went on to college –
and Bobby joined the Marines.

He completed basic training –
and came home to say good-bye.
Then left for active duty –
to a place called Vietnam.

Soon he was in-country –
in the province of Quang Tri.
On patrol in heavy rain –
the devil showed his face.

His platoon was ambushed –
overrun by NVA.
Bobby was killed in action.
A tragic end for a gallant man
trapped in a faraway land.

I stood with his family at the airport
when his body came home in a box –
covered by the flag of his country.
A sad exchange for what he gave up.

Was he a hero or a pawn
for the political machine?
He was my friend – that much I know.
I think of him often and wonder –
what would he be doing today?

His death, lost in a cause undefined.
A big why with no answer.
A void still waiting to be filled.
His life over before it really began.

Wasted potential -
a young man in his prime.
Victim of a misguided government.
What was the meaning and purpose?

I went to his funeral.
There by the gravesite I stood.
I heard the salute of the guns -
and the sound of taps on the hill.

I looked at his family
so heavily burdened with grief.
Their spirit damaged and broken
the loss of their son was too deep.

An officer presented his mother
a flag in a triangle fold.
Lifting her head, she replied:
Sir, is this all I get?

Our lives will continue
but they won't be the same.
Farewell brave soldier.
Farewell to my friend Bobby Gainz.

Brothers of the Sword

Rows of granite headstones
stretch far beyond the eye.
I walk among the fallen
who lay beneath the grass.

Yellow flowers neatly placed
in designs that speak of peace.
No one famous rests here
just soldiers from the ranks.

Battle sounds I hear
from lands so far away.
Few can tell the story
of how they met their end.

No arms were there to comfort them
when they trembled from the fear.
Their thoughts were not of glory,
but of loved ones to be near.

Their final words silenced
by the raging sounds of combat.
Their souls placed by God
in the hall of fallen heroes.

Cannon stand in silence now,
the bugle calls them home.
May they never be forgotten
these brothers of the sword.

Sin of the Cloth

Today the flames burn high in hell,
reaching up for Catholic Priests –
men of God who betrayed their flock.
They preyed upon our children –
These sick demented beasts.

Mighty Bishops bear great guilt,
for they looked the other way.
Refusing to acknowledge –
they all hid them away.

Young lives forever damaged –
by these disgusting deeds.
The Church now stands divided
losing members just like leaves.

Struggling in decline -
many doors are boarded up.
Congregations bow their heads
in dishonor and disgrace.

David Mello — All Smiles
Coupland TX, 2015

.

Made in the USA
Middletown, DE
02 March 2020